The Sensational Woman

Learning to Embrace and Love Your Greatest Asset... You!

By Cathrine James

ISBN 978-0-9864165-9-0

Published by The Legacy Project
2018
Printed in the United States

TABLE OF CONTENTS

To my brother.
You left this world before I could finish the book.
Here's your copy.
I love and miss you.

Acknowledgments

I would like to express my deepest gratitude and appreciation to my amazing Godsend of a husband, who encourages me to leap and has supported every wild idea and business venture I've ever started. You are much more than I could have ever dreamed of. I love you so much.

Thank you to my children, who have graciously taken the ride with me. You two are my inspiration and reason. I love you dearly.

Thank you to my parents for doing the best you could with the information you had. God does not make mistakes! I love you both.

Thank you to Laptop Publishing, Mwale and Chantel. If it had not been for your prompting, this book would have remained inside of me a bit longer. Thank you for a seamless experience.

Thank you to all of my clients and the women who entrusted me with their growth process. As you learned from me, I learned from you. To those of you who purchased this book, thank you. I pray that your life will be blessed beyond measure and the words on these pages will give you the courage to release the stories that no longer serve you and grab hold of the sensational life that awaits you!

Last but far from least, I thank my Lord and savior, Jesus Christ, for never leaving me, for keeping me through it all and for using me as your vessel to show others how to love and embrace their greatest asset. There are no words to express my love for you.

Introduction

We enter this world fully prepared and gifted to live out our purpose. We are equipped with the skills, mind, physical stature, and power needed to be exactly who we were created to be and to do exactly what we were created to do. We enter this world pure and without judgement; without judgement of self and without judgement of others. While walking down the street the other day, I passed a father and his two young children, who if I had to guess were two and three years of age. As we passed one another the children waved happily and said "hi". I smiled and said "hello". Upon looking up to make eye contact and speak with the father he stared right past me, never attempting to make eye contact or acknowledge me. I thought, how interesting, the children in their unaltered and pure state had no problem acknowledging others. The father, was a different story.

Unfortunately, for the vast majority, life's experiences- both good and bad, can reshape us and take us off course. After speaking with hundreds of women and examining my own life, I have found that after years of abuse, disappointment, struggle and listening to the opinion of others, our original design that was powerful, confident and once allowed us to acknowledge and accept others without judgment, takes on new form. One that is unfriendly, lacks confidence and is controlled by what others think. One that hides behind bad attitudes, success or titles, makeup and designer clothes.

I am guilty. At one time or another I have hid behind each of those things simply because I was off course. I did not understand that my very existence was an asset to this world. An asset is something that provides a positive return in the future. When we are created we are given everything we need to produce a positive return in the future. We were created to be assets. However, because we discount our worth, we fail to see ourselves as the assets that we are. The time has come for that to change! The time has come for you to get back on the course that was laid out for you. Before you go any further you must make a commitment to yourself; a commitment that you will take the steps and do the work needed to return to your authentic self, utilize the skills, mind, stature and power within you to be who you were created to be and learn to love and embrace your greatest asset...YOU!

MY COMMITMENT

I commit to taking the steps and doing the work needed to return to my authentic self.

I commit to taking the steps and doing the work needed to utilize the skills, mind, stature and power within me to be who I was created to be.

I commit to taking the steps and doing the work needed to learn to love and embrace my greatest asset...ME!

_____   _____
            Signature   Date

I would recommend that you copy and keep a copy of your commitment with you to reference it when you find yourself returning to old habits. As you will find from the pages in this book, learning to love and embrace all of you is a journey. Let's embark!

Chapter 1: Rediscovering Your True Self

As a child I suffered a great deal of pain. This pain stemmed from various forms of abuse, including physical abuse, sexual abuse, verbal abuse and emotional abuse. As I scan the nooks and crannies of my mind in search of the happy times of my youth, I am challenged to recall times of true bliss beyond the age of four. Nonetheless, I am thankful for these childhood memories.

The mental picture that comes to mind is that of a little girl with a big afro playing outside all alone. I did not have siblings or animals at the time and was often found playing with dirt, bugs and imaginary friends. Despite the voids, that four-year-old little girl was happy and joyful without a care in the world. My parents lived together, but I do not ever recall sitting or spending quality time with them. I do not recall them being present or taking the time to speak life into my young mind or world. As I think back, I have no idea how many days I sat outside playing alone on the steps of that apartment building on 23rd Avenue in Oakland, California. What I know is that no matter how many days it was, they were good days. Days when I was allowed to operate as my true self, days when life didn't matter, days when my mind and spirit were free and peaceful.

Shortly thereafter, my parents separated. My mother moved away from the apartment complex on 23rd Avenue, and my life began a trajectory that would forever change my world as I knew it. The move to School Street was a turning point. From age four I lived between both my mother's and my Nanny's house, as children whose parents are divorced and sharing joint custody often do. During the school year, I was with my mother a few days during the week and with Nanny a few days during the week. I spent most weekends at Nanny's house. During the summer I was with Nanny nearly seven days a week and visited with my mom occasionally.

My elementary school was across the street from my mother's residence. It seems as though I was walked to school by my mother when I was at her house, but the details are faint. More clear to me is the transformation that took place within me at that time. The moments I remember are when the blissful four-year-old turned into a worried, afraid and uncertain five-year-old. The shift was as fluid and as transparent as the change in seasons or my change in age, four years old to five years old.

> "Life is a succession of crises and moments when we have to rediscover who we are and what we really want."
> - Jean Vanier

Who Is Behind Door Number 1

In May of 2008, I was asked to speak at a women's conference titled "Who is That Lady?" The weeks leading up to the conference required me to go into a space of deep reflection and listening. Before developing any speech, I always pray and ask God to give me a message for those who will be in attendance. The content of the message rarely presents itself right away, so I pray and I wait. While waiting to receive content for this particular conference, I found it humorous when a song released by the Isley Brothers in 1964 titled "Who's

That Lady" came to mind and was suggested for the opening of my speech. I anxiously began to wonder what was to come next. The next and the rest of that message was not at all humorous to me. In dealing with the question, "Who is that lady?" I discovered I no longer knew who I was. My very identify had morphed from an independent, self-sustaining woman who had dreams and goals to "his wife" and "their mother." My husband and children drew their own attention. My husband and son are both outgoing and charismatic. My daughter is more like me, more of an introvert and quiet, but she has the most loving spirit and is cute as can be, which drew people to her. My identity was now deeply intertwined with my familial titles. As I prepared my speech, I found myself thinking, "People don't even know my name." They don't address me as Cathrine. Instead, it is usually, "Oh you are so and so's wife," or "You are so and so's mom." I would have been the first to admit that this was never a bother before I started preparing for that conference and was forced to ask myself, "Who am I?" That became the title of my message: Who am I? That question was followed or answered by the words: I am all that I am.

It occurred to me that I was not the only woman who faced this issue. It is a known fact that many women put everyone and everything before themselves. In an effort to be the best wife, mother, daughter, sister, etc., women sacrifice themselves and their dreams to please others. We wear that sacrifice like a badge of honor until the day comes when we have to face the music and dance to the song "Who's That Lady." In looking at my life, all I could see were doors, doors with titles such as wife, mother, employee, business owner, church member, daughter, friend and sister. Doors that I would gleefully enter and exit at any given moment as needed, doors that would one day feel as though they were smothering the woman God created me to be.

Does this sound familiar? When was the last time you stopped and asked yourself, "Who am I?" When was the last time you gave yourself permission to take time to think about yourself and assess your own happiness? I know what you're thinking: "Of course I'm happy; I love my family," or "Of course I'm happy; I have a good job." These really aren't the same thing, though. It's very possible to have a wonderful, loving family and still feel unfulfilled. It's possible, and very common, to have an objectively good job and still feel that you're not living up to your potential. You're not alone, and I encourage you to listen to that voice or your intuition the next time it speaks or the next time you get that feeling in your gut. Don't just push it aside. You know yourself better than you might think, so don't discredit any internal feelings of discomfort; they're there for a reason. You owe it to yourself to examine those feelings and find that reason. So, who are you? If you're not the woman that you want to be, then where is she?

I examined my world looking high and low for the woman I knew I was meant to be. I knew she was not gone. I knew she stood behind door number one waiting for permission and the appropriate time to open the door. She was the woman who was polite and powerful, serious and sanguine, graceful and gracious, forgiven and forgiving. She was the very essence of the words "I am all that I am." The woman who stood behind door number one had to cultivate and grow before she could emerge. She had to learn to love everything about herself: her full lips, big behind, sandy red hair, velvety voice and freckled face. She also had to learn to love the pieces of her that were not so obvious, the things that brought her pain, guilt and shame. Things such as the one-night stand, the abortion, the promiscuous behavior and the miscarriage. She had to learn to love her uniqueness, her no nonsense disposition, analytical thinking, strong will, bounce back ability and internal strength. She was put together a little different in comparison to the majority of her family members and friends. Her internal rhythm caused her to dance to a different beat. Rarely participating but always observing, she purposely stayed out of the bright lights to watch others and gain an understanding of her gifts and purpose. The woman behind door number one sat patiently but worked fervently to accept her stuff and love herself, to ensure she was ready when the time came for her to gracefully strut through the opened door.

In order to better present the journey that led me to where I am today, it is important that I present and examine some moments and memories from my past that have not only stayed with me but affected me deeply and taught me throughout the years.

The Lost Child

One of my earliest childhood memories involves getting separated from my mother at a department store. "Sit right here, don't move from this spot. I will be right back," my mother said as she quickly vanished into the crowd of Macy's Christmas shoppers. Macy's was not a store we frequented, in control of the situation. No child should have to feel this way. No child should experience this kind of terror at such a young age. However, the sad truth is that many of us have. Many of us were forced to grow up much earlier than we ever should have had to. So many of our experiences are outside of our control and not up to us. What is up to us is how we move forward. We must not let our experiences or our circumstances define us. We are so much more than that.

It Won't Leave Me Alone – The Rediscovery Journey

The next year we moved again, this time to Paxton Street. New friendships were established quickly. It was on Paxton Street that my purpose was first revealed. I still recall rising early on Sunday mornings before my mother—when I was at her house—to get dressed for church. I found joy in dressing up and wearing my "church shoes." I would wake up early, as this was my time to perform on stage at the Paxton Street Theatre. After getting fully dressed, shoes and all, I would mentally transform my bedroom into an auditorium and my bed into a stage. It brought me great pleasure to look out into the audience at the hundreds of people who had come to have their hearts and minds transformed.

At the time no one could have convinced me I would one day be a speaker. I was sure I was going to be a singer. My performance consisted of me flailing my arms and pretending to be Lynette Hawkins, while belting out the words to the gospel song "Be Grateful" by the late Walter Hawkins. Pondering the words of that songs brings a smile to my face. "God has not promised me sunshine, that's not the way it's going to be, but a little rain, mixed with God's sunshine, a little pain makes me appreciate the good times. Be Grateful." How is it that a child, at such a young age, would choose a song with such powerful words? It is as if God was not only showing me what I would do but also preparing me for what I would go through. A little rain and a little pain.

The rain and pain over the next few years would turn my make-believe auditorium and stage back into a bedroom and bed. It would no longer be a place for me to pour into the lives of others, but a place for me to retreat and ball myself up into a fetal position as I searched for comfort. The multiple events that would occur in the coming years would cause me to forget about encouraging others and make me believe I was no longer worthy of being used by God. I would become the damaged soul I once envisioned I would help helped me believe my purpose was for me.

Everyone is created for a purpose. It is God's desire for all to live abundantly. The trials and tribulations of life often cloud people's vision and will sometimes make them give up on their dreams. Those trials and tribulations really do become your testimony, and the pain becomes your preparation. Diamonds do not start out as the sparkling, shiny precious stones people gladly spend thousands of dollars on. Diamonds are hidden underneath the earth's surface in kimberlite, a molten rock. The rock has to be crushed in order for the rough diamond to be revealed. Once revealed, the diamond has to be sawed, chiseled and ground to become the beautiful gem people admire. The diamond goes through a process before it reaches it's purpose. Albeit painful, we too must go through a process before reaching our purpose. Like the diamond, our true beauty is uncovered during the process. The most important thing to remember is that while God shapes us, He walks with us. He carries us through the darkness and rejoices with us in the light. Most importantly, once the diamond has been formed, it must be shared. In the same way, once we have been formed and realize our true purpose, we must share it with the world. Our unique gifts and talents enable us to fulfill our potential, but these are gifts and talents that must be shared with others. If we realize and embody what brings us joy and gives us life, shouldn't we lead others to do the same? Don't let the diamond stay hidden.

> "...I come that they may have life and
> have it abundantly." - John 10:10

Chapter 2: Appearance vs. Reality

"If you are that grown, you don't need a daddy," were the words he harshly spoke through the receiver in response to the pre-teen verbal lashing and critique I had given to express my dissatisfaction with his parenting skills. I was twelve. His words were quick, as if he was ducking one jab while throwing another. That certainly wasn't the reply I was looking for. After that conversation, it would be years before I spoke to my father again. Prior to that telephone conversation, he had never expressed anger towards me. On the days he made unexpected visits or I happened to be outside playing as he passed my Nanny's house on his way home from work, he made me feel as though I was the most important person in the world.

Regardless of his absence in my life, I had a special kind of love for my father. Although I didn't know it then, I now know his absence was a result of a drug addiction that helped him cope with the pain of losing his parents as a child and being moved around from one foster home to another. His only role model showed up when he was sixteen. It was this man who taught him the ropes of life and how to be a man. At least, that's what my father believed as he was introduced to all the wrong things, including drugs. Even though he had this sickness, when he came around he was always pleasant and in good spirits.

Since we had moved away from northern California two years earlier, I no longer experienced his occasional surprise visits or sightings. We no longer spoke on the phone, because I was sure his words meant he didn't love me anymore. What father would say such a thing to his firstborn and only daughter? I found myself perplexed by the situation but deep down believed it was my mouthing off that caused the strain and erased my place in his heart.

Things are not always as they appear, which can be so hard to remember but is vital to understand. My father's behavior had nothing to do with me and everything to do with him and his unresolved issues. He harbored deep-rooted pain that not even he understood. Early disappointments in life along with one bad influence would place him on a long road to self-destruction. He would find himself parked on streets called Victim, Anger, Venom and Worthlessness. His view of the various street signs would take him further and further away from his family, those who loved him and his purpose.

He was gone from my life. I believed it was my fault. Rather than face the truth of how his absence left a void, I chose to act as though he had dropped off the face of the earth. Pretending he didn't exist allowed me to remove thoughts of him from my mind. As stated, I have since learned the truth about the reasons for my father's actions throughout the years. However, as a child, I didn't know his story. I didn't know he was a hurt, disturbed and confused young boy when he fathered me at sixteen. Much of his story has been learned over the course of the last few years after he was snatched from that hell pit and placed on roads called Sobriety and God's Forgiveness. I am thankful he woke up before it was too late.

His wake up call came in the form of a heart attack almost four years ago that literally took his life twice. His heart was restarted by the EMT's defibrillators, only to stop again and require additional shocks to restart it and revive him again. Since that experience, he has remained sober, and I have had the pleasure of moving from appearance to reality. It appeared as though he did not care about me; however, in reality he loved me but did not love himself and therefore could not show me love. Today he has turned his life over to Jesus. He continues to work through his issues and is a beautiful soul. Our conversations, which are almost daily now, are authentic and full of laughter. There is not a day that goes by when I do not receive an email or text from him telling me how much he loves me.

How do appearances line up with reality in your life? Examine the relationships in your life. Examine your relationship with yourself. What are you holding on to that's preventing you from growing and moving forward? Working to gain a deeper understanding of the people in your life can move you towards repairing broken relationships or clearing up ancient misunderstandings.

We Wear Makeup When We Really Need a Makeover

By age nine I was enrolled in a school near Nanny's house and was living with her nearly full time. Every morning upon waking I would shuffle through the house in search of Nanny. She could always be found sitting at the dining room table peering at the words in a gigantic, large-print, white Bible, the kind that was too heavy to move let alone carry to church. I remember nearly every house we visited had a gigantic, large-print Bible someplace out in the open, mostly on dining room or coffee tables. I am sure most of them were for show but not Nanny's. Hers was worked overtime. She studied her Bible for hours every morning. It was her practice to wake and begin her studying before the sun or her great-granddaughter would rise. She was a devout believer and lived her life accordingly. Nanny will continue to be a very important person in my story, as she shaped my life in very formative ways.

She spent very little time dressing up or making up her exterior unless it was Sunday. On Sundays she made a little more of an effort, maybe a little lipstick and blush but nothing elaborate. Nanny was naturally beautiful and could get away with wearing no makeup. She may have known this, or she may have been hanging on to the old religious belief that it was a sin to wear makeup. Whatever her reason, it was obvious that she felt it far more important to work on the inner being as opposed to the outer. Our neighbor a few doors down, on the other hand, was the exact opposite. She was absolutely gorgeous. I always thought she could have been a model. However, she would spend hours making up her face to present her flawless exterior to the world. She would not be caught answering the door without having made up her face. If she did not have makeup on, she would not open the door.

Nanny was a peaceful woman with a peaceful spirit for the most part. Her feathers were rarely ruffled. If they were ruffled by chance, she would call out, "By Django's!" To this day I am not sure where that saying came from but I know it meant she was "vexed" and I or somebody else was in trouble.

This inner peace that I saw in Nanny was not something I saw in my beautifully made-up neighbor who kept to herself and had very few visitors other than her male "friends." The difference in the two women was best described by a minister who told of how women get all made up on the outside to hide the pain on the inside. Nanny spent time getting made over internally while our neighbor spent time getting made up externally. Whether that minister was the first to discover the correlation between external makeup and internal pain is unknown to me, but since hearing this interesting stance I have found it to be true more often than not. The more makeup, the more pain.

I witnessed this observation to be true for our neighbor. Once, while I was at her house during a rare visit, she must have really needed to talk to someone. She allowed me to enter and sit down. Over cookies and whatever she was drinking, we sat and talked for at least an hour. She talked and cried to a nine-year-old as if we were the same age. Of all the things she said, there was one that struck a chord: "She deserved to be treated badly." An internal makeover was needed. Unfortunately, I continue to see women like my neighbor, women who are made up and absolutely stunning on the outside but oh so flawed on the inside. Too much effort goes into hiding the flaws as opposed to accepting them or dealing with them by way of a makeover.

Makeovers take work and time. Again, Nanny read her Bible every day for hours. Makeovers require honesty; one has to admit he or she has pain. Makeovers take courage, the courage to face your struggles over and over again until you gain control over them. If I were teaching my daughter about the concept or importance of external beauty versus internal makeovers, I would reach back to Nanny as a model. I would tell her to feed her spirit on a daily basis. I would tell her to admit the hurt and seek help. I would tell her she is not alone and has nothing to be afraid or ashamed of. I would tell her to find the good and the lesson in every situation. I would tell her to forgive those who inflicted pain upon her. I would tell her the pain will remain until it is examined. I would tell her it is dangerous to wear makeup when she really needs a makeover. And just as I would give this advice to my daughter, I give it to all of you. Don't hide from your mistakes; learn from them. Don't cover your scars or your bruises; let them be an unabashed part of who you are and who you will become.

Loving Life

In my adult life, it took years for me to honestly say I loved life. Oh sure, I had the best husband a girl could ask for. He truly was and is my knight in shining armor. My children were delightful and brought joy to my heart, but I also had painful memories from my past that attempted to define my present and future. Not all of the pain was a result of my past, though. Some of that pain was current pain.

The term "functional alcoholic" is used to describe a person who, despite his or her abuse of alcohol, somehow manages to keep his or her life in order. For a long period of time in my adult life, I could have been described as someone who was functionally depressed. Similar to the person who drinks too much and continues to hold life together, someone who is functionally depressed continues to hold life together despite remaining in a state of depression for a period of at least two years. It is difficult to recognize someone who is functionally depressed because he or she goes to work daily, interacts with others and smiles while in public. However, this person is always sad and has no hopes or dreams for the future. This person performs the duties of life that must be performed but longs for the time when he or she can retreat to a space occupied by only him or herself. This act could go on for years because the outside world sees a freely functioning person. The person suffering may not even be aware of the functional depression because, again, he or she appears to be handling life.

Each day after work when I arrived home I would walk past my husband and children, only briefly exchanging greetings, and make my way to my bedroom. Once there, I would drop my things on the floor, fall onto my bed and burst into tears. This had become so routine that my husband and small children knew to stay out of the room. They knew to leave me alone until I came out. Sometimes I would lay there and cry for 15 minutes, and other times it was much longer. At some point after my meltdown had run its course, I would get off that bed to deal with my family and life again. I knew my family was worried about me, and I hated causing them any distress, but I couldn't help it. My thoughts and my emotions during this time were outside of my control and more powerful than I fully realized at the time.

I don't know when I slipped into that mode of life. I believe life caught me off guard. There was so much I did not know about life, and the on-the-job training was more than I could handle. I don't know how long I remained in that state, and I don't know exactly when things changed, but I know and I am thankful that I was kept safe during that time and was brought out of that state. Because of the magnitude of that experience, I can tell the story, and I thank God that today it is nothing more than one of my stories. The emotions associated with those days are long gone. The journey through this emotional state and my subsequent recovery took a lot of self- examination, forgiveness and prayer.

The rest of these pages will explore my journey towards loving life and the lessons I learned along the way.

During times of struggle, I drew a lot of comfort and wisdom from things Nanny used to say to me. "Just because you slip and fall in dung doesn't mean you have to lay there and wallow in it," was a Nanny-ism. This statement began to play over and over again in my head. Some days I believed that Nanny and her wise words had come to my rescue. The words "clean yourself off and start over" would follow. Her simple instructions, "clean yourself off and start over," became my life jacket and not only gave me hope but also filled my mind with questions. Questions such as, 'what was the dung in my life and what did I need to do to clean myself off?" Although I had worked through the state of functional depression, I still wasn't fully happy. I still wasn't living up to my full potential. I still wasn't using all of my gifts and talents in the way I knew I could. As I thought about Nanny's words, I decided I would follow her example. I rose before the sun and my family to read my Bible and create lists, lists of things I wanted and things I didn't want. Each desire brought freedom and strength. I eventually reached a point where I focused only on what I wanted and who my creator said I was. I realized I had forgotten who I was and what I could do.

When I shifted what I thought about and started dwelling on the fact that I was wonderfully made and had unmerited favor, I could feel the blades of grass under my feet even during the times when it felt as though I was walking on stones. In assessing my situation, I found that things were not very different than they were when I was operating from that functionally depressed state. The primary change was where my mind sat and how my thoughts had changed to include more optimism and positivity. I believe there was a divine intervention to pull me out of my previous depression. However, because of my life calling, I knew I did not have the right to stop where I was. I was in a much better place, but I still had a long journey ahead of me. I still had a lot of goals to achieve. I believe this realization to be true for everyone. The journey is ongoing and remaining stagnant doesn't help anyone. Although there are always challenges along the way, these challenges and how we rise to meet them make us who we are. Everyone has challenges. Our challenges become our championship stories that we use to connect with those we were created to help, encourage and inspire. What are the challenges that made you who you are? Have you reconciled these challenges into your story? They are a part of you and cannot be left out of your story if you ever wish to heal and move past them.

A Thorough Cleaning

"Do not conform to the patterns of this world, but be transformed by the renewing of your mind. Then you will be able to test and approve what God's will is. His good pleasing perfect will." Romans 12:2 NIV

From 2003 – 2007 I tried my hand at my second network marketing business. I was a follower of Robert Kiyosaki and was invited to hear him speak. The conference I attended was called FED or Free Enterprise Days. During this conference I heard and saw so much more than Kiyosaki. I learned the meaning of free enterprise, listened to people speak about how their lives had changed after becoming business owners and learned of a monthly subscription that allowed people to receive personal development materials. Within a week I was a new business owner, not because I wanted to make money but because I wanted that monthly subscription. I thought that subscription would be a great way to hear about and receive new books.

I got exactly what I was looking for out of that experience. Although I hit all kinds of personal goals and won contests for trips, I never made any substantial money with the business. What I got out of that experience was something more valuable than money: a renewed mind. Being a part of that organization allowed me to tap into the thoughts of people who weren't afraid of going after their dreams, people who believed that there were no limits and people who amassed various levels of success. They were different than the people in my circle of influence, and I liked it! The person I became as a result of that experience was drastically different than the person I was when I began.

FED, which was once a year, would become my favorite conference. One year, my then mentor and up-line told a story about a bowl of muddy water. He spoke of how the only way to clean the muddy water in the bowl was to pour clean water in the bowl on top of the muddy water. He stated that you would have to continue pouring the clean water into the muddy water until all of the muddy water was gone and there was only clean water left in the bowl. The illustration was used as an analogy, with the bowl of muddy water representing our minds and the clean water representing the information we could put into our minds to change our thinking. This illustration of the water assured me that working on my mind and thoughts was imperative. The quote by Bob Proctor and Lisa Nichols, "what you think about you bring about," was on my mind a lot at this point. I read James Allen's book *As a Man Thinketh*, which only further emphasized the need to focus on my thoughts. I turned to the Bible and Proverbs 23:7 told me, "For as he thinketh in his heart, so is he." Everything I read, everything I saw, seemed to contribute to this fixation on improving my mind and sorting through my thoughts.

I was fortunate in that I never had a victim mentality. I never questioned why my life had started out so rough; I just questioned whether or not I had the ability to attain the life I dreamed of living. I grew up in the inner city, was supported by the government and lived in low income housing units. Today I praise my mother. She was a very young mother and had three children by age 26. She did the best she could with the information she had, but I did not want to continue down that path of codependency. She told me if I wanted nice things I needed to get a good education so I could get a good job. I had heard this enough to know that if I worked hard I could buy nice things, which was okay for a while, but I learned quickly that "stuff" was not going to buy me peace of mind. It would take years of mental examination and cleansing before I would reach that place of mental freedom where I understood the power I have and that things will happen in life but I get to choose how I respond to those things. It would be a while before I understood that expectations can lead to disappointments because I can only control myself. It would be a while before I understood that God has equipped me with all I need to be who I was created to be.

It is said that God operates in mysterious ways and in His own time. It can be one thing to know this on a fundamental level and another thing entirely to understand it on a personal level. As I mentioned there is so much power in outlook and attitude. We get to choose how we react to what happens to us. When we choose how to react to situations, it also affects those around us. Our actions have power. While we are only in charge of ourselves, we do hold responsibility for how our actions will affect other people. Therefore, choose wisely. Choose patience. Choose compassion. Choose understanding.

Chapter 3: Lone Ranger

Perhaps it was because I was an only child until the age of six or perhaps it was the ridicule and verbal lashings that taught me how to live in a safe internal corner, a corner that kept me alone even if I was in a room full of people. I grew up being told, "Children are to be seen not heard." I took this to heart, and as a result my voice was silenced. Unfortunately, it was not only silenced to avoid disrupting the nearby adults but was silenced to all. The insecurities, lack of confidence and feelings of insignificance would not allow me to speak up for myself when necessary. As a result I was an easy target for the bullies at Warren Lane Elementary in Inglewood, California. I can still remember the names of some of the girls who excluded me from the double-dutch games, talked about my hair and clothes and called me the ugly duckling.

My mother moved my siblings and I from Oakland to Inglewood in the early 80s. She had been in a long-distance relationship with a man nine or 10 years her senior. She said she always wanted to leave Oakland and saw this move as an opportunity to do just that. The move presented multiple unpleasant predicaments for an 11-year-old girl who had just been uprooted and torn away from her Nanny, the one person she knew loved her and she loved back unconditionally.

Up until this time, I practically lived with my great-grandmother. To the great-grands she was known as Nanny. For me Nanny was the very air I breathed. Due to the young age of my parents when I was born, Nanny became my primary caregiver and took care of me while my mother attended school. She was the only person who made me feel as though I mattered all the time. She was the only person who showed me what unconditional love looked and felt like. She was my everything, my protector, my encourager, my teacher, my judge and jury, my disciplinarian, my healer, my everything! It all changed one summer day in 1981. An eight-hour drive from northern California to southern California expanded my once safe internal corner into a now safe internal house. Without Nanny on my side, I became more withdrawn and kept to myself a lot. I felt like I was on the outside looking in. I wanted to belong, but I was now out of my element and in very unfamiliar territory.

Other than the neighborhood boys, I had no friends. While at school I would often sit on the bench watching and wishing I could play with the other girls who had already developed a bond and saw me as the new girl who didn't act, dress or look like them. When I wasn't sitting on the bench, I could be found inside one of the classrooms doing extra work. This became the norm, as it was during these moments that I was at peace. There was no one to judge me, no one to ridicule me, just me and my thoughts. This was also the place where I further developed a comfortable but dangerous coping mechanism, isolation.

I was misunderstood by my peers and clung to myself for comfort. I didn't think I needed other people. I didn't think I wanted other people. However, by our very nature, humans crave contact. We crave connection. We crave understanding. My isolation became so dangerous because I had cut all of those things out and internally denied that I'd ever needed or wanted them. As you'll see, this didn't work out to my benefit.

The Dangers of Isolation

For the most part, I had gotten along well doing things on my own. I learned early in life that I had to depend on myself. Nanny was the exception to this philosophy. When I found myself in a bind or in need of loving words, Nanny was there. However, Nanny's dementia became progressively worse over the next few years. She had dementia at 69 when I still lived with her, but no one had ever heard of dementia so we just thought she was acting strange. Before things got really bad, she and I spoke on the phone daily for hours at a time. She was my best friend. I know she was busy and had her own life, but she always had time for me. I knew I was something special to her. She knew she was something special to me. When she departed from this world, first mentally and then physically, for a long time thereafter I felt as though I had no one. I lived on her words and Nanny-isms, many of which, I now know, were scriptures from the Bible.

With her physical absence, I lived off of her words. "Baby, you can do anything you want to do and don't you let nobody tell you different," she said. These words gave me such strength throughout my life. Nanny believed in me even when I didn't believe in myself. I missed Nanny so much, and remembering her words was like carrying a small piece of her around with me.

William H. Johnson said, "If it's to be it is up to me." This was my life's motto. I had been let down so many times that I trusted no one but myself after Nanny died. Despite rarely having someone on my side, I forged on to conquer the ills of the world and create the life I desired to live. It was on or near my 21st birthday when I laid out a plan for my life and created solid deadlines. By the age of 25, I wanted to be married, own the car of my dreams and purchase my first house. This goal became my primary focus. No longer was I interested in spending my Friday and Saturday nights at the club. No longer was I interested in short term relationships. I had a goal to achieve, and I only had four years to make it happen.

My friends did not understand the sudden shift in my behavior, and to their defense, since I failed to share my plans with them, their lack of understanding was reasonable. I couldn't blame them for being confused. Unfortunately, my shift in focus and their lack of understanding caused a wedge to develop between us. There came a point in time when I was excluded from discussions regarding group events or outings. After a while, not only was I excluded from discussions, but I was also excluded from the friend circle entirely.

Being excluded from my friend circle bothered me, but I was on my grind and trying to make life happen. Instead of trying to make amends, I put on mental blinders, put my head down and returned to the internal house of isolation. Instead of trying to repair friendships, I began to develop a plethora of ideologies about why I did not need anyone. I reasoned that as long as I had Jesus I didn't need anyone else. This underlying ideology was tucked away in my mind and showed up whenever I felt the looming presence of disappointment or hurt. Although this ideology brought me comfort, it also kept me from developing authentic relationships with anyone outside of my immediate family.

I did attain my goals. By age 25 I was married, had a nice car, owned my home and had a son. However, there was one problem. Other than my husband, who I loved and enjoyed tremendously, there was no one to share my happy moments with. Over time life became very lonely. I longed to be part of something again. I began to think about the past more and more. Don't get me wrong, I had several long-time friends who would drop everything and come to my rescue in a time of need and vice-versa, but I now longed for the closeness, the laughter and girl time. I longed for the regularity of those weekend hangouts and adventures. I missed my friend circle and wished I could have a do over. I wished I hadn't shut them out when my priorities shifted. I wished I had let them in and shared my thought processes with them. I wished I had asked for their advice and brought them with me for the new phase of life I had sought. Unbeknownst to me, my isolation had become my suffocation. I thought it was the right way to approach things. However, the very thing that once protected me and kept me from the cruelties of the external world had begun to slowly and softly kill my internal world.

Power of Community

Despite attending church regularly and growing up hearing about the importance of my church family, I had become accustomed to being alone and doing things on my own. I was a go-getter. Whatever I set my mind to, I made happen. My salary had reached six-figures; I owned and operated a small but profitable real estate company; I sold jewelry and started a Life Coaching business. Life was good. I was crazy busy trying to manage it all, but life was good, or so I thought.

It was only a few months ago when I had to face the pain of being a lone ranger. Yes, I knew I missed having girl time and the ability to pick up the phone to share with someone other than my husband, but that was my norm. I had become used to it. As I always say, "It is what it is," or in this case, "It was what it was." What I needed and was missing in my life was more than just a "girl time" kind of friend. What I was missing was a community of women or people that thought the way I thought, that saw life the way I did and that loved and supported one another's dreams and goals from a cellular level. A community of women where everyone was rooting for one another's success, praying for each other's families and sending love and encouragement across the miles. A community that presented no drama, jealousy or envy, just grown women who had found their places in life and desired to leave the world better than it was when they came. 15 years ago, during one of my many multi-level marketing ventures, I was blessed to have such a community. Unfortunately, many of the relationships and the community fizzled when I moved on to other ventures. It was great while it lasted, but I needed more. I needed a longer lasting community. This community from 15 years ago gave me a taste of what I had been missing, what I had been looking for.

Isolation doesn't serve anyone. Introspection

and contemplation evoke positive connotations. Self examination is very important. Isolation, however, can be very dangerous. I learned this the hard way. Isolation can bring about a crushing loneliness that can be paralyzing. In order to fulfill your purpose, you have to be content with who you are and at peace with where you are. This peace is very difficult to achieve when you're trapped inside your own head all the time.

A short time after this realization, I had a sudden rush of emotions, and my eyes filled with unexpected and uncontrolled tears as I stood in a hotel conference room talking with a more seasoned entrepreneur whom I had come to admire. Her words, "You will be alright, you just need a few more powerhouses to run with," burned like rubbing alcohol being poured onto an open wound. Where in the world did those tears come from? Why was I having a minor emotional meltdown in the middle of the floor in a conference room while speaking with someone I hardly knew? Her words were truth, and as Nanny would say, "The truth will set you free." This woman, even though she really didn't know me, could clearly see that I needed more companionship. It was obvious, even to an outside observer, that I needed an extended support system. I needed some "powerhouses" to bounce ideas off of, talk through ideas with and be part of a community with.

Like other times of contemplation and searching in my life, I found a lot of solace in scripture. Hebrews, in particular, had some powerful insight about the importance of relationships and community. Hebrews 10:25 reads, "And let us not neglect our meeting together, as some people do, but encourage one another, especially now that the day of his return is drawing near."

It is no coincidence that the book of Hebrews encourages us to continue meeting in an almost demanding way: "and let us NOT neglect our meeting together, as some people do." The statement is very clear and places emphasis on the importance of a community. It commands us: do not neglect meeting together. We are to not only get together but we are to encourage one another as well. Community is essential. In any line of work, in any stage of life, we all need people to be encouraged by and encourage in return.

After our opportunistic meeting, I took that woman's words to heart and found a few more "powerhouses" to run with. These women have been such a blessing in my life, and I am so grateful for this positive change. We support and encourage each other, and we understand each other. We know the struggles that we all face and celebrate in each other's successes. I am loving my newfound community!

If you don't have a group of "powerhouses," I strongly suggest making that a priority. It is such a blessing to have a group of likeminded people to place your trust in and be supported by. It's impossible to be unbiased about our own lives, and a community reminds us of our achievements when all we can see are our failures. A community helps us know when to push ourselves and when to pull back. Most importantly, a community draws us outside of ourselves and towards something greater.

Super heroes/heroines are For Entertainment Only

It's funny what memories remain over the years. Especially when we can't really control what sticks and what doesn't. I can still remember the words to the Enjoli Perfume commercial: "I can bring home the bacon, fry it up in a pan and never let you forget you're the man. I can work till 5 o'clock and read you tickety tock and love and kiss you... cause I'm a woman, Enjoli." The tagline was "an 8 hour perfume for a 24 hour woman." There's a reason I remember this commercial. It felt as though this commercial reshaped the way women were to conduct themselves. Soon after this commercial, women could be found striving to bring home the bacon and fry it up in a pan. Somehow it was felt as though this behavior made them better women. While there were not many women in my low-income community who modeled this behavior, my Aunt Aunita showed me something different. She was the Enjoli woman. She was the only person in our family who had a corporate job and owned her home. As far back as I can remember, she lived life on her terms. I admired her and desired to one day accomplish what she had accomplished. She was a positive role model among the many tough relationships in my life.

As I entered my adult years, I came to understand that while she made it look easy, my aunt's road was not easy. Following in her footsteps, I would come to endure some of the same struggles she endured: being talked about by family members, struggling to pay bills, picking up the slack for everyone and everyone attempting to diminish your accomplishments. I remember she would joke about Captain Save a Ho, frequently reminding people she was not Captain Save a Ho. To put things in perspective and help you understand my aunt, I will say Tyler Perry's character, Madea, has nothing on her. Her "Captain Save a Ho" comment is mild in comparison to the plethora of sayings she has and spouts out freely. She speaks her mind, and while I admire her for that, I am sometimes shocked by what comes out of her mouth.

Although she joked, when it came to our family she was Captain Save Them All. After Nanny died she became the matriarch of our family. Her tiny, size-five feet had to fill some big shoes, which she did with ease. She was there with her cape to save the alcoholics, the drug addicts, the homeless and dysfunctional adults who refused to be responsible for their lives and stand on their own. Now at 70 years of age, she continues to wear her cape, providing shelter and food for whoever is in need. Over the years I have watched her cape lose its color and become frayed. It was Spiderman who said, "With great power comes great responsibility." My aunt has owned both her power and responsibility.

There is a part of me that often wonders about the price she paid and continues to pay to wear her cape. I am quite familiar with the strain and heartache that comes as a result of achieving a little bit more success than those close to you. Not realizing you have your own challenges and issues, those closest to you are quick to lean on you and seek you out in their time of need. The weight gets heavy, but fearing I am the only resource, I simply pray and ask God to give me the strength I need to keep going. How I wish I had the power to spin around as Wonder Woman and become a superheroine. How I wish I had the ability to change my outfit in a phone booth, only to come out with supernatural powers that would allow me to solve the problems of my world. Wonder Woman, Superman and all the other superheroes are great for entertainment purposes only. Real superheroes and superheroines do not have a quick fix at their fingertips; they have to endure the good with the bad. They have spiritual and internal strength to draw from when needed. They know that they do not need a cape or supernatural powers to save the world; all they need is an ability to show love and kindness to those who are in need.

As simple as this may sound, you must give yourself permission to be successful. You must give yourself permission to use the gifts and talents that are inside you. Unlike Superman or Wonder Woman, your "powers" do not come from some mysterious supernatural source. They come from God, and with Him on your side, you cannot fail.

Chapter 4: Fear Factor

In the summer of 2001, I'd rush into my house and turn on the television to catch those opening lines: "I'm Joe Rogan, and this is *Fear Factor*." The rush of adrenaline in anticipation of what was to come next would nearly immobilize me. *Fear Factor* was one of the first reality television shows. Despite the fact that I did not watch much television, I would willingly give up an hour of my time on a weekly basis to anxiously watch and see the next stunt. *Fear Factor* was a show that challenged contestants to face their fears. Weekly, contestants were petitioned to complete stunts such as eating sheep's eyeballs, drinking pureed rats, lying in a locked chamber with snakes and jumping out of flying helicopters. Some of the stunts were so repulsive I would be forced to turn away from the television. No matter how nerve-racking the stunt though, I would sit there glued to my seat in front of the television for the entire hour.

What I am aware of today is that it was not the stunts that hijacked my attention; it was the contestant's willingness to take action in the face of fear. There was a huge incentive of $25,000 for the winner or the person who successfully completed all of the stunts, but I would venture to say that those who were afraid but took action anyway also won. Perhaps not the money or tangible prize, but they won a piece of their soul. They knew what they were made of. This was my reason for returning each week. This was my reason for giving up an hour of my life. I felt inspired and courageous after watching the show each week.

There were many areas in my life where I failed to take action because of fear. At that time I would not return to college for fear of not understanding or being able to keep up, I would not change careers for fear of being judged because I didn't have a college degree and I would not take financial risks for fear of losing the little money I had. I allowed fear to keep me imprisoned to a life I knew I did not want. So, for an hour each week, I would sit in front of the television and draw from the boldness and courage of the contestants.

Despite my growing understanding of fear, I still had and have fear because it is a natural emotion designed to protect us from harm or danger. The problem is that the emotion is unable to decipher between real harm and perceived harm and therefore shows up not only when there is real danger but also when there is perceived danger. When our mind perceives change or something new as dangerous, it goes into protection mode. Fear tells us we are in trouble when we are doing or considering something new. In that moment the mind must determine whether it is going to be controlled by the fear emotion and flight response or if it is going to go after what it wants and fight through the instinct to protect us from perceived danger.

According to the Psych Central website, "The fight or flight response is a sequence of internal processes that prepares the aroused organism for struggle or escape. It is triggered when we interpret a situation as threatening." One's handling of the fight or flight response is what separates those who thrive in life and those who dive in life, those who control their fears and those who are controlled by their fears and those who live and those who exist. We all experience fear. For me *Fear Factor* was so fascinating because it was a visual example of the fight or flight response. There were the contestants who were able to push past their fears and fight through to victory, while the others succumbed to their fears and ran from them. I was so intent on watching the show because it resonated with what was going on inside me. Within me that very fight or flight struggle was taking place, each instinct battling the other to win out in the end.

How large of a role does fear play in your life? Do you let it control you and make your decisions for you? You cannot let fear, fear from your past or present carry over into your future. Often, we are afraid of something simply because we don't understand it. Examine your life and your choices. Remember that fear is a natural instinct in the face of danger but can be a serious impediment when there is only perceived danger from a new situation. Look back on your life. What if you had listened to fear every time you were anxious about trying something new? You would have never done anything! Now, look at what's been possible when you were able to push past that fear and move forward anyway. You will want to listen to that voice. The voice that admits you're afraid but that in the end it's going to not only be worth it but you will also be okay.

What Are You Afraid Of

Scientists believe nearly all fears are learned and contend that we are only born with two innate fears: the fear of falling and the fear of loud noises. It is believed that most all other fears, natural fears, are learned (CNN.com – What is The Science Behind Fear). The fear of dogs, learned, the fear of bugs, learned, the fear of poverty, learned, the fear of success, learned, all learned at a young age. I found this school of thought to be very interesting and began exploring my own fears: the fear of how my success would affect those closest to me, the fear of failing and the fear of no security. As I thought of where my fears may have taken root, I began to agree with the scientific findings. These fears were all learned. However, where my fears came from was far less important than the fears themselves.

Many of my clients and staff members have expressed fears or concerns about what others think of them. Anyone who has been around me long enough knows I do worry about what others say or think of me (been there done that, it didn't work), and I often tell clients, friends and family, that what others think of you is none of your business. During a really hard time in my life, I had to release the fear of what others thought of me to keep my sanity. I determined I was creating additional hurt and being abusive toward myself by worrying what others were saying or thought of my situation. "Sto' bought sense is the best kind," was another Nanny-ism. In other words, learn from experience. Experience had shown me that worrying about what others thought of me did not make a difference in my life; it did not add value to me or my life. So during that time, as a logical person there was a need to make my thoughts make sense to me. The best line I could come up with was if someone wasn't contributing to or paying my mortgage then his or her opinion did not matter.

This adaptation in thought would come to be my strength during many more situations. In other words, if someone did not have a direct impact on my life or any direct involvement in things I needed to survive, then I shouldn't live my life according to their opinions. I needed to live my life in a way that made sense to me. If someone didn't like that or judged me for it, then that was their problem, not mine. After all, it was my life, not theirs.

Far too many people sit down on their hopes and dreams because they are afraid or concerned with what others will say. How is it that we are more concerned about others' opinions than our own? Others are no better off than you. They may paint a different picture, but remember that everyone has their own struggles. If we let what others think stop us from achieving our dreams, then nothing would ever get accomplished. There are always going to be people who disagree with your ideas and opinions. There are always going to be people who dislike you. You really can't please everyone, but you don't have to. It is far worse to try to please everyone and let your dreams fall to the wayside than to ruffle a few feathers and be your own person in the world.

My fears were actually created in my mind. My calling was revealed to me years ago. What was revealed did not line up with who I saw myself as or what I believed I was capable of doing. Rather than jump completely into my possibilities, I would simply dip my toe in. I knew fear was present, and I lived behind excuses like lack of time, family or children's functions, when the hard truth of the matter was that I was insecure, afraid of failing and afraid of asking for help (I will address this in depth later).

For many years I did not know how to handle failure. I somehow believed there was some correlation with failure and who I was as a person. I had heard and believed failure was a bad thing all of my life. I did not want to have that associated with me. I now understand that failures aren't really failures at all; they are learning experiences. When you can learn from a situation, be it good or bad, it is a learning experience, and learning experiences are always good. The key is to learn from every situation. I was able to stop playing small because I was no longer afraid of failing. You can and will want to view every experience as an opportunity for growth. Use what you can and discard or file what you can't. There is some truth to the saying, "All things happen for a reason." I slowly came to realize that it was better to try something and fail at it then to never try at all.

Have No Fear

Growing up I loved to watch cartoons, which were much different than the cartoons of today. Many of the cartoons back then were in faded color and included animals such as the dog, Scooby Doo or the coyote, Wile E. Coyote. Often the story lines ushered me into my imagination, where I found myself heroically capturing the bad guys or mentally solving mysteries. One of my favorite cartoons was *Underdog*. Other than the show's opening line, "There's no need to fear; Underdog is here," and the little dog himself, I don't remember much more about the show. There was something about the opening line that was exciting to me. It seems as though I could somehow relate to being the underdog in life. Though not the smallest in stature, I usually felt I was the smallest when it came to being significant or important in comparison to my cousins or the other children in the neighborhood. I was usually afraid of being different and not fitting in, which was often because I *was* different. Think about it; I spent the majority of my time with a 70-year-old lady. I had an old soul. I didn't care to play games or ride bikes. Although I preferred to sit in the house and read from my collection of Bible story books or watch shows like *Hee-Haw* and the *Gong Show*, I would force myself to do what the other children were doing in hopes of fitting in.

Fitting in was not only a challenge because I was different but also because I was away most of the time at Nanny's, so I was unable to invest the same amount of time building relationships as the other children. I often felt like Underdog and often had to tell myself, "There is no need to fear." However, it is impossible to have no fear. As stated earlier, fear is a natural emotion. A better line for me may have been, "Don't become stuck because of fear." To deny that fear exists is to deny being human. Instead, try doing what I did. Try coming up with your own mantra about fear, but one that is realistic and attainable. Acknowledge that fear does exists, but it doesn't control you or define you.

My mother did not know fear, or at least that was what I thought. She is an extrovert, very outgoing, and no one is a stranger to her. She can strike up a conversation with anyone as if she has known the person for years. She didn't recognize this trait as a gift but someone else did. My mother's "Jafra Lady," as she called her, convinced my mother she would be a great at selling skincare and makeup products. My mother in turn became a "Jafra Lady" and she was great at selling. During the first few months, she broke sales records and was acknowledged for her accomplishments. Because operating in your gift requires little energy, my mom didn't think much of her accomplishments and was often heard saying, "I am just out having fun and talking to people." Her "fun" increased her income substantially in a short period of time. This development was great until the time came for her to meet with her Section 8 worker and report her income. My mother and her Section 8 worker attended the same church. Because my mother sold Jafra to fellow church goers, her worker was aware of the additional income. My mother, having no idea she was supposed to report her side income, completed her Section 8 paperwork as she usually did, reporting only her regular income which was very little. During the meeting her worker told her she wanted an account of her side earnings as well because she needed to count it as income. A second meeting was conducted after the additional earnings information was reviewed. It was at this meeting that my mother was told she was making too much money to qualify for low-income housing. She would no longer receive the government's assistance if she did not stop selling Jafra. Based on her sales history, she was on track to make more money than she had ever made in one year, but she would never know what could have been because she abruptly stopped selling for fear of losing something she clearly no longer needed. Where could she have gone, how could she have changed her life had she not allowed fear to get in the way? So many times we miss our blessings due to fear. We either never take action or only go so far because of fear. We must get better at reminding ourselves not to become stuck because of fear. This example from my mother's life stuck with me. I didn't want to miss out on an opportunity like she did with the Jafra venture.

Fear or Pride?

The lines between fear and pride can sometimes become blurred. I was proud of my accomplishments. As a result of a strong work ethic and determination, I had achieved things no one else in my family had achieved. I had six direct reports and 45 indirect reports. I was the Assistant Manager overseeing the account of a large public entity. I had not yet attained my degree and did not meet many of the preferred qualifications, but my manager knew I was capable of doing the job and recommended my promotion. Her belief in me elevated my belief in myself. It also made me work even harder in an effort to gain a full understanding of my role and the expectations of both my internal and external clients. I was intentional about improving my leadership skills. I attended leadership conferences on my own. I read leadership books and spent ample time learning from my manager, who had also become my mentor. I had a great relationship with my external client and was proud of it. Thereafter, with each new position and each new accolade, I was proud of my abilities and results.

Merriam-Webster defines fear as "an unpleasant often strong emotion caused by anticipation or awareness of danger." Pride, on the other hand, according to *Merriam-Webster* is "a feeling or deep pleasure or satisfaction derived from one's own achievements." Pride in this definition appears not to be a bad thing, but Habakkuk 2:4 says the soul of a proud man is not right within him. It is clear to me how both fear and pride can cause one to become stagnant. Fear keeps you still because you are afraid to take action; pride keeps you still because you are reliving old actions.

While attending a Speak and Write conference in Atlanta during the summer of 2017, an exercise revealed to me that it was fear that had me stuck. During the VIP session, we were instructed to partner with another person. We were to ask each other one question: "What are you afraid of, or what is your lie?" One person was to ask the question; the other person was to answer and then switch, where the person answering was now asking. We were to repeat this process over and over for a specific length of time. The purpose of the exercise was to speak your fears or lies. About mid-way through I said, "You will never leave Corporate America," and burst into tears.

Again, I was so confused by the sudden emotion. What was going on here? Where did those words come from? I had reached beyond the surface and found a fear I didn't know was there.

After pondering, I determined that I had been stuck not only because of fear but also because of pride. My fear and pride were working hand in hand. Pride was protecting and masking fear. Pride was telling me I was making a good living, I had done well for myself and if I didn't achieve my dreams and goals at least I had done more than most. Pride had created a comfortable and unrecognizable spot for fear to reside.

"When you know better, you must do better," is what Nanny would tell me. I felt it was time to do better. The truth had been revealed. Fear and pride had blocked my path. Knowing better than to believe either, I returned home and jumped into action. Were fear and pride both still present? Yes, but they could not affect me as they had in the past. I now had a plan. I knew what my obstacles were and it was time to start overcoming them. This was the time to move forward on my path.

Throughout the years I found that it is either fear, pride or sometimes both that have prevented me from moving forward. Often times my mind would create pretty stories such as, "You are doing well; it doesn't make sense for you to put yourself out there even further and lose your anonymity," to keep me in a safe place. The problem was that I knew better, and because I knew better, I had to do better. I had to choose purpose over both pride and fear. I had to push past my comfort zones and past where I felt safe. I knew I was created for more, and it was time to start listening to that.

On their own pride and fear are not bad things. They are normal and, in the right context, healthy. As discussed, fear ties to self-preservation. Pride, though in a different category, is just as important. If we do a good job on something, we are entitled to be proud of our work. It is normal and healthy to be proud of our kids, our spouse, etc. However, be wary of letting either stop you in your path like they did with me. Don't be too proud of a situation to change it if it no longer yields fruit. Don't let fear of the unknown stop you from making a change if one is needed. Taking steps towards fulfillment is always the right answer, however hard it may be at the time.

Chapter 5: Lies We Tell Ourselves

Like fear, lies can be used as a form of protection. However, unlike fear, lies are not a natural physical reaction. Lying is a conscious decision. Most people tell lies to avoid negative consequences, such as the child who is dishonest about breaking mom's favorite vase. Sometimes people lie to gain an advantage of some type, such as the embellished résumé submitted to obtain a position for which one is not qualified. When one thinks about lies being told, I would guess most would reflect on lies being told to others. I don't know that the thought of telling lies to oneself comes to mind.

It is my belief that the true you shows up when you lay down to go to sleep at night. It does not matter if you are alone or someone is lying next to you; it is at this time that you are alone with your conscience, and your conscience shows you the real you. No matter what you tell others, you always know the real truth. For the sake of this writing, those little white lies that make you out to be more than who you are are not the lies I am referring to. The lies I am referring to are the lies that are created unconsciously. These lies are the lies that take place between your ears and play without permission. These lies or this chatter is the noise that goes on in your mind all day and says things like, "You can't do that, you are too old, you need a college degree, they are smarter than you, you are not good enough, you deserved it, you missed your window of opportunity, you've invested too much time to leave, you've done enough," etc. These are the lies that somehow discourage you and give you permission to remain in a place you have no desire to be in. Too often, people miss the great things in life because they fall for the lies.

Prior to meeting my husband, I was sure my boyfriend at the time was my soulmate. The fact that he had two children (I had none) and a baby momma did not deter me because, aside from that baggage, he was good to me. We had fun together and could talk to one another about anything. I had fallen in love not only with him but also with his girls and his mother. There were many red flags throughout our first year and a half. The largest of them all were the wedding pictures I found while snooping through his things. My mind went into protection mode and the lies started. *He loves me too much to lie to me about such a thing, they must be divorced.* Upon his arrival, I began to question him about his marital status. In turn, he began to question me about snooping through his things. After the initial round of questioning, he admitted that he was married but wanted a divorce long ago. He just didn't have time to pursue it because of his work schedule. Since I had previously done paralegal work with dissolutions I was quite familiar with the divorce process and volunteered to complete his paperwork for him.

The lie that kept me operating in this pitiful state was that he was my soulmate. As lies go, one lie usually creates another lie. I began to create one lie after another to make things right in my mind. The divorce papers sat on the table for weeks without his signature. His excuse was that he was too tired when he got home. My lie supported this and told me that he does work long hours and has a very arduous job. When his wife started showing up to his house unannounced and hostile, my lies told me she just wanted him back. Even though she told me they had gone out a few times, I could not hear her, because I was too busy listening to my own lies. Looking back now it's so obvious what was going on, but my lies were shielding me from the truth. It's amazing how easy it is to fall for the lies when the truth is right in front of you. We are not objective observers in our own lives.

This now silly story illustrates how we can become so engrossed in our lies that we fail to see the truth. The truth about life is that every day that we are allowed to open our eyes and breathe air is another opportunity to go after our dreams. No excuse is good enough to make you sit down on your dreams. You can do it. You are not too old. Depending on what you want to do, you may or may not need a college degree. Others may have an advantage in that they have more information than you on a given subject, but no one is "smarter" than you. You are good enough. You deserve it. You will only miss your window of opportunity if you leave this earth before taking action; no matter how young or old you are, your whole life is in front of you!

I'm an Overachiever

I can't count the amount of times someone has called me an overachiever. I admit I felt some sense of accomplishment when I was called an overachiever or asked the question, "How do you find the time do it all?" At one point in life, doing it all meant being a straight-A student, taking ROP classes after school, running track, being Captain of the Tall Flag squad and taking care of my siblings. At another point doing it all meant parenting two teenage children, being a wife, working full time, managing our rental properties, running a coaching practice, taking online classes to obtain my degree, starting a youth organization and attending all events for my children. Being all I could be and doing all I could do was how I thought I was to live my life.

I was highly focused on the end result, and it was my goal to reach the result as quickly as possible. Deep down inside I knew this drive and deep longing for achievement stemmed from some other deeply rooted issue, but I refused to address that issue. After all, this overachievement behavior (I did not consider myself an overachiever) was working in my favor. I had accomplished a lot and proved so many wrong. I was not stupid. I was smart. I did amount to something. I had accomplished as much as I had without a college degree. In fact, my friends who had degrees called on me for help with articulating their thoughts or determining how much tile would be needed for a 15X20 room. I relished this; I was everything people said I had no chance of becoming.

University of Rochester psychologist Andrew Elliot said, "Overachievers have an underlying fear of failure or a self-worth contingent upon competence." He further said, "Rather than sitting and striving for goals based on a pure desire to achieve, their underlying motivation impels them out into the world to avoid failure." Avoiding failure was my motivation, and I am sure my self-worth was tied to some aspect of that chaos. However, buzz words such as results oriented, perfectionist, organized and go-getter were how I defined myself. There is nothing wrong with that; who would not want to be those things? However, everything must have a healthy balance. Resting is a part of a healthy balance and is as important as being driven.

As I sat in the doctor's office waiting to see a cardiologist after experiencing ongoing heart palpitations, I didn't imagine she would tell me that the cause was sleep deprivation. While answering a series of questions about my lifestyle, I began to face my chaos and question why I felt the need to be everything and do everything. Prior to seeing the cardiologist, I was operating on four hours of sleep per night. I woke up every morning at 4 AM and went to bed every night at 12 AM. I had full days that I thought I was managing well until my primary physician referred me to a cardiologist. This scared me, but the conversation with the cardiologist scared me even more. She advised that I had borderline hypertension and required medication right away. I was healthy and had never taken medication for anything, so I surely did not want to start taking medication for high blood pressure. I was too young for that anyway. After a few visits, I was able to bargain with the cardiologist by promising that I would take my blood pressure at home every day to ensure it was in normal range and I that would get at least six hours of sleep. She acquiesced.

That cardiologist scare was the beginning of the end of my overachievement ways. In addition to changing my sleep pattern, I sought out the assistance of a life coach to help me disrupt the lies that were put upon me by adults and children during my childhood. Lies such as, "You're not good enough," when I was the last person picked for the kickball team or the slew of negative insults I heard on a regular basis. Lies such as, "You're not smart enough," when I was scolded for an incorrect answer or called a stupid bi_ _ _ for throwing a spoonful of rice in the trash after dinner. Lies such as, "You're not going to do anything with your life," when I was caught kissing a boy in elementary school. These and many more lies affected how I felt about myself. Being an overachiever was like putting tracing paper over the lies. They were covered but could still be seen. After removing the tracing paper and exposing the lies for what they were, there was no longer a need to be an overachiever. I am still driven and have full days, but now I can laugh at myself when I do something wrong. I often refer to myself as a recovering perfectionist; I don't freak out when I'm not first, and I give myself permission to slack off sometimes. I have a balance. I understand that I can't just go all the time without ever stopping to rest. Success is measured in so many different ways; it's not just about how much you can accomplish in a day. Success also looks a little different for everyone. A healthy and balanced life looks different for me than it's going to look for you. However, no matter who you are, balance between your personal and professional life is absolutely essential. Without it, your life can become all or nothing one way or another.

Loyalty (Staying Too Long)

A while ago, I was more than confident that I had overstayed my welcome in the industry, but I reasoned that I should stay because it was my career and I had been doing it for eight years. My mind told me it was better to stay with what was familiar. It was all I really knew how to do. I was good at it and my peers were telling me I was would be crazy to leave such a lucrative job. Perhaps my unhappiness was temporary? I pushed my thoughts to the side and decided to focus on becoming better in my job. Maybe if I invested more of myself, I would feel a larger sense of accomplishment. While I was able to find comfort in my decision for a period, it did not last long.

I am reluctant to report that that discontent was 19 years ago. Today, although I am building a business and I have been a Personal Development coach for nine years, I have to admit that loyalty kept me far longer in my career than it should have. Those thoughts I pushed aside would return every couple of years, and I would create a new plan for comfort. Instead of seeking a larger change in my circumstances, I focused on smaller details, hoping that if I gained control over them I would be happy. This cycle would continue until I got intentional about doing what I was created to do. The fact that I remained in the industry was not what caused the periodic nudging in my soul; it was the fact that I was operating outside of my calling. Whenever I redirected my focus away from my calling and placed it solely on my career, those uneasy feelings of selling my soul would reappear.

For years I believed it was all or nothing. I would either go to work every day or build a business. I believed that my day job was a distraction, as the job itself was stressful and required a lot of energy. This meant that unless I returned to the overachiever I promised I would not be, working during the day and building at night seemed impossible. That is, it seemed impossible until I got off the all-or-nothing wagon. I had to shift my perception of the situation in order to move forward. When I decided to build slowly but consistently and to focus on the lives I was touching rather than on growth, the windows of heaven opened up. When I broke the goals down into smaller tasks, they suddenly became achievable. I didn't have to accomplish my dreams overnight; I just had to take it one day at a time.

I have spoken with many who found themselves unhappy with their day jobs but were unwilling to do anything different. Some of the stories mimic mine in that they've been at their jobs a long time or they don't have any other skills or they make good livings. We allow ourselves to become stuck because we are loyal to a process, routine or an organization. There is nothing wrong with this if you are content and you enjoy what you do. You are encouraged to continue doing what you do. However, in contrast, for those who know you have stayed too long because of loyalty you are encouraged to ask yourself, what would happen if you were loyal to yourself first? What would happen if you were loyal to you before you were loyal to your job, before you were loyal to your kids or before you were loyal to your spouse? What would happen? Would you really stay where you are? Or would you be willing to make a big change in order to feel fulfilled?

The example I used pertains to a job, but staying in any situation too long when you know you have long overstayed your welcome and you fail to make any adjustments will suck the life out of you. This advice applies to relationships as well, whether romantic or friendships. When life is sucked out of you, you can no longer live how you were created to live. You can no longer perform at peak levels. You feel defeated; you find yourself complaining about small things and all your days look the same. This is not the way life was meant to be lived. All of our days aren't supposed to look the same.

What would happen if you were loyal to yourself first? You would add value to everyone and everything around you. You must be careful not to operate from a selfish space, though. You want to operate from a selfless space. There is much talk today in the workplace about loyalty programs and the benefits of loyalty programs. Some of the benefits noted in an article found on Marketing Land's website include: proven to boost growth, inexpensive, improve your reputation and make customers happy. These benefits apply to personal loyalty as well, not just corporate. When you are loyal to yourself first, when you take care of and nurture yourself first, you have so much more to give to others, and you can partake in some of the same benefits noted. Being loyal to yourself first will cause you to grow personally. People will admire you for doing what so many others struggle to do, and your employer, family and friends will appreciate the value you add to their lives. When you are happy with your life and your choices, you can help others towards their own happiness as well.

Get More

The American Dream! I wanted it and was sure it would make me feel successful. Growing up on the heels of the baby boom generation, all I heard about was the American Dream. It sounded so exciting! My mother's teaching was that if you want a good job, go to school to get a good education. Due to life's circumstances, I sought a job over college. At 18 my mother and I did not see eye to eye on hardly anything, and I could feel the tension levels increasing. I had taken several college courses toward an associate's degree at the community college before dropping out. I'd thought I wanted to become a computer programmer and had taken a few programming courses. With a limited education, my options were few. I thought I had enough knowledge in programming to land a job in that field. I quickly found I was being a bit too optimistic. I was happy to receive a call from a recruiter who said a firm wanted to interview me to run their computer department. That would be my entry into the world of corporate America and path to my American Dream. The job turned out to be a glorified data entry position. When people had problems with their computers, if turning it on and off didn't solve it I would call IT in the corporate office, who would verbally walk me through the correction process. Despite the somewhat mundane duties I performed, I loved what I was doing. I loved the company, and I made enough money to get a roommate and move out of my mother's house. These steps towards independence were really important to me. I was on my own and supporting myself now.

Things were good, but I was far from my American Dream. An avid learner, I began to take courses in preparation for a promotion. A year or so later I received a promotion and was sent to Atlanta for three weeks for training. The American Dream was closer but not yet within reach. I continued to take classes and obtained a state license. In the meantime, as I was working towards all of this, I also got married. Four years after starting with that company, my husband and I received the keys to our first home, a small, two-bedroom, one-bath house that was 910 sq. ft.

It had worked. I followed the instructions, got a good job and got my piece of the American Dream. My American Dream would soon turn into an American nightmare, though. I had all the glitz and glamour but no money. I worked to pay bills. In an effort to improve our situation, I started this perpetual spiral of getting more: more education and more stuff, more education and more stuff. A bigger house, European cars, private schools and personal trainers. I was stuck in this mentality that more was better. It seemed that the more we had, the better we were doing. I did not think I had time to attend a university or obtain a degree, so I attained one certification after another. Despite all of these steps towards certifications and education, we were still struggling. My husband returned to school for his master's, and I eventually returned for my bachelor's. After it was all said and done, we had gotten more and more in search of a way out of the nightmare only to find ourselves in an even deeper sleep from which we were unable to awaken. At the time it was very overwhelming. It felt like there was no way out of this situation.

Getting more was the lie. I thought if I got more I would have the means to eliminate more. This was not even remotely true. What I learned was that getting more is encouraged to fuel the economy and add to the assets side of the bank's balance sheet, but for me "more" added to the liabilities side of my own balance sheet. More was not the answer. Instead, reviewing my life and developing a strategic plan to change my life for the better would become my answer.

I adopted a new way of thinking and a new way of living. I would not let society define my dream. I now know that just as people have different dreams while sleeping, people can have different dreams for life too. Owning a home and fancy cars, paying for private school, etc. was a part of my plight. In the moment, even with the struggles, it felt right. In hindsight, had things been done differently, I would have focused more on creating assets rather than liabilities. I would have focused more on being a lender as opposed to a borrower. I would have evaluated the long term effects of more. In the long run, was "more" going to yield a worthwhile return on my investment? Importance must be placed on what you're getting and how it will affect your life 10 years from now. Get more of the things and people that will make deposits in your life long after you made your initial investment.

What does the American Dream look like to you? Never feel bad about yourself because your dream does not match up with someone else's. Never feel that you need to explain or defend your dream to those who disagree with you and place value on very different things in their lives. Just as the dream looks different for everyone, the achievement of that dream also looks different. Success looks different. As I learned, "more" is not automatically better.

Chapter 6: Purpose Driven Life

While attending a seminar, I heard Les Brown say, "You were created on purpose for a purpose." Those words resonated with me and returned to my thoughts multiple times as I drove two hours from San Diego back to Pasadena. By the time I arrived home, the words had changed to, "I was created on purpose for a purpose that was purposely designed just for me." The minor alteration pricked my soul and took me back to the mornings when I sat studying the book by Pastor Rick Warren titled *The Purpose Driven Life*. It has been many years since I read that book, but the one chapter I've never forgotten is the chapter titled "Living with Purpose." I understood that everything I had gone through, the good, the bad and the ugly, was about my purpose. I understood that being the great-granddaughter of Annie Lou Diggs (aka Nanny) was a part of my purpose. I understood that my very birth was no accident but a part of my purpose. I understood that being born to the parents I was born to and enduring the many forms of abuse I had suffered were not random occurrences but all a part of the purpose I was created for.

When I accepted that none of it was about me and instead was all about how God would use my experiences to help others, I was able to view my life totally differently. It took a while to get there, though. I would question, "Why me?" and, "How?" but then I would question what gave me the right to think I should have been preserved and excluded from going through what I had gone through. Spiritual maturity stopped me from questioning the bad and directed me to a passage in my favorite book that says, "And we know that all things work together for good to them that love God to them who are called according to his purpose" (Romans 8:28).

I believed those words from Romans and had been told them most of my childhood; I just did not see the good yet. I walked by faith for a number of years, believing something good would come out of my life. I believed my purpose would call me to women who had also experienced traumatic moments in life and were stuck spiritually, mentally, emotionally and physically. These women would be mothers, business owners, employees, wives or single, but all would have a common thread called "stuck." Women who, despite their various levels of success, were unable to release the thoughts and effects of their traumatic experiences. With my own experiences, I would be able to help these women work through their challenges and make sense of their struggles. Since I could relate on a personal level, I knew I would be able to be a credible source of understanding and support. I was someone who would really and truly be able to relate to their experiences.

I came to understand that my purpose was about helping others to heal and go on to lead rich and rewarding lives. My purpose was about providing hope to the hopeless, encouraging the discouraged, and helping fix the broken. My purpose was about helping women heal from the inside out. I would learn that the women would look and act like me. No one would know of or hear her silent cry. No one would know of her secret sufferings, and no one would know of her hidden hurt because she believed she had to present an image of perfection. Because of my experience with functional depression in the past, I would be able to truly understand what these women were going through and how much pressure they felt to keep it all together and maintain an appearance of togetherness. My purpose was to reveal to these women what redemption looked like and it was to help them uncover their purpose. We all have a purpose. Life's events are all a part of our purpose. You were created on purpose for a purpose that was purposely designed just for you.

Society's Story

According to statistics, my life should look very different. It is said that children born to teen parents are less likely to succeed. The American Academy of Child and Adolescent Psychiatry reports that children born to teenage parents "are at risk for long term problems in major areas of life including school failure, poverty and physical or mental illness." Urban Child Institute reported that "children born to teen parents are less likely to reach their full potential, hinder a child's social and emotional welbeing, have more difficulty acquiring cognitive and language skills." Lastly, the Centers for Disease Control and Prevention (CDC), reported that "children born to teen moms are more likely to drop out of high school, become teen parents, use Medicaid & CHIP, experience abuse/neglect, enter the foster care system, end up in prison (sons), be raised in single parent families, 9 times more likely to be poor if the mother did not finish high school and is unmarried and have lower vocabulary, math and reading scores."

The statistics do not stop there. There are also statistics about teen parents. In addition to the statistics, and probably more damaging, is the backlash and harsh treatment teen parents, primarily moms, receive from those close to them and strangers alike. Comments such as, "You are too young," and, "What a shame," are heard regularly. Looks of disgust, disappointment or pity are flashed their way in passing. Friends are lost when friends are forbidden by their parents to continue the relationship. Teen parents are expected to fail. They are expected to drop out of school. They are expected to live in poverty. They are expected to parent at subpar levels.

The school I attended for high school was referred to as the pregnant school because it was the designated school for all pregnant teens. If a teen's pregnancy became obvious while attending one of the other high schools, she was required to leave that school and enroll in the pregnant school, where a parenting class replaced her extra-curricular or elective class. The school had two campuses. The pregnant girls attended most of their class on one campus, away from the non-pregnant students. I am sure the district believed that it was looking out for the best interests of the soon-to-be young mothers, but it does not appear that the young girls' feelings or self-esteems were ever considered.

Teen years are difficult enough for the average teen. It is a period where teens are already trying to fit in and discover who they are. It is a period where friends and a sense of belonging are very important. Many of the pregnant girls who were forced to transfer schools lost those things when they were removed from what was familiar and placed in an unfamiliar environment with others who were isolated. They lived with implications that they were not fit to attend school with "regular" teenagers. What effect did these implications have on their self-esteem; what did this do to their psyche?

As with all other stereotypes, children born to teen parents, and teen parents themselves, are labeled and defined as a group rather than as individuals. Statistics capture past trends based on past behaviors. Not all who fall into these categories produce the predicted results. Past trends and statistics can be changed with new behaviors. If it is possible for one to perform better than expected or predicted, it is possible for all to perform better than expected or predicted.

You are not a statistic. You are a unique individual that cannot be lumped into a set of numbers and trends. The danger comes in when you allow yourself to be defined by your circumstances. Regardless of your background and upbringing, if you allow yourself to think that you are going to turn out a certain way because of environmental factors, chances are you are going to turn out that way. In order to break free from the mold and shatter the numbers, you have to take agency over your life and make the choice to live with purpose. This leads me to my story and how I fit into the statistics.

i) *My Story*

Although I managed to escape many, unfortunately I was unable to escape all of the statistical predictions. Yes, I was raised in a single family home. Yes, for the majority of my years at home we lived with some form of government assistance. Yes, I nearly became a teen parent myself. However, I have never struggled with vocabulary, math or reading. In fact I loved these subjects, and I finished high school on time with an overall GPA of 3.5. I believe my story was different because of the information that was poured into me. I believe I was equipped differently. I somehow was able to use both the derogatory comments and mistreatment combined with Nanny's sweet, loving and kind treatment as fuel to unknowingly break the stereotypical chains. Instead of succumbing to the difficulty of my circumstances, I rose above them. I refused to be part of the statistics; I knew it didn't have to be that way. I was determined to become everything people said I would not and everything Nanny said I would. I longed for the day to prove them wrong and to prove her right. My will to succeed, albeit an unhealthy reason at the time, would create a life that few could have predicted.

Contrary to my will to achieve was my ability to laugh and enjoy life. Sometime during my youth I had lost my ability to laugh. My childlike spirit had all too quickly taken on adult roles. I thought it was just the way I was. It never occurred to me that my feelings had been numbed as a method of coping with life. I was forced to grow up too quickly, and as a result, there were consequences. At a young age I had seen and heard too many things to maintain the childhood innocence I should have been able to keep for much longer than I did.

At the age of six I started taking care of my siblings. After my brother was born, I assisted with changing his diapers, making his bottles, rocking him to sleep and whatever else he needed. My duties and responsibilities increased as he aged. He soon became my shadow and went nearly everywhere I went. I would become to him what Nanny was to me. When my sister was born the cycle repeated. Now 10, I again was placed in a role for which I did not audition. As with my brother, I assisted my mother with changing, feeding, clothing and bathing. Unlike my brother, her hair had to be combed daily unless my mother braided it for the week. I would also become to my sister what Nanny was to me. There wasn't much time for me to be a child; my mother and my siblings needed me. By age 10 I was more of a maternal figure to my siblings than I was a friend or playmate.

From six to 18, with limited knowledge and resources, I attempted to provide my brother and sister with something I longed for: unconditional love, quality time and support. I had a very special and close relationship with my brother and sister. I was their sister, but due to our age difference, I acted more like a mother. I taught, disciplined and rewarded as I saw fit. Some of my fondest memories with them were the days I would take them on field trips to Chinatown. They had to earn these trips by either getting a good grade or completing their chores. Because I did not have a car, we traveled by way of the city bus. There was a bus stop near our home. We would leave the house early in the morning, take a 30-minute bus ride and get off right in the middle of Chinatown. We would walk around entering and exiting one shop after another, touching and playing with various trinkets. The owners did not follow their patrons around the store in those days. We roamed freely with little money and no intentions of purchasing anything. On good days we would share fried rice at one of the local restaurants. Other days we would eat the snacks I'd brought from home. Before boarding the bus to return home, we would always stop at the store to purchase sweet and sour dried plums. They were a small treat that we all enjoyed. They always brought a satisfying end to our field trips.

I moved out of my mother's house for the final time at 19. I first moved out at 18 but had to return because the woman I was renting a room from decided she no longer wanted a roommate. By 19 I had landed my first full time job with benefits. A friend and I agreed to live as roommates to minimize our expenses. From 19 to 22 I lived my own life. I had a plan and a schedule. Monday through Friday, other than an occasional visit from a male friend, I was about business. I would go to work and then back home daily, spending my evenings talking on the phone (texting had not yet been invented). The two people who I did not speak with often enough were my siblings. At the time I felt as though this was part of my way of finding air. Again, I had been responsible for my siblings since age six. I just needed a break. I didn't resent them or anything like that, but for the first time in my life, I had independence. I wasn't in charge of taking care of anyone but myself.

Two evenings out of the week, I attended rehearsal for either my church choir or a local gospel group of which I was a member. Friday and Saturday nights were spent with my girlfriends, clubbing, drinking and enjoying life. I felt as though I was beginning to find myself. I was beginning to breathe. Throughout all of this, my faith remained very important to me. My relationship with God had gotten me through a lot of tough times in the past, and it continued to do so in my young adult years too. No matter how late I stayed out Saturday night, I could always be found in church on Sunday mornings. By 22 this young adult phase of my life was over. I was no longer looking for a good time. I was done with the club scene and the weekend binges. I wanted more. I wanted substance. I was ready to move on to the next phase. I was ready to begin my grown-up life. For me the next phase of life would involve meeting my husband, getting married and starting a family.

God's Story

The one thing both Nanny and my mother had in common was church. Both attended church religiously. Nanny was one who had to be there every time the doors opened. She went to church a minimum of three times during the week and all day Sunday. My mother, rain or shine, could be found in church every Sunday. Their practices made it so that I too was in church frequently. I am not one to complain about being in church every day of the week. In fact, I have a great appreciation for both my mother and great-grandmother for bringing me up in the church, for church is where I gained a greater understanding of God's love for me and the scriptures. My knowledge of the scriptures is what has kept me going over the years. During times of struggle where I didn't know where else to turn, I always found comfort in scripture. Although I did not always know who I was, I was always keenly aware of whose I was, and that meant there were promises made to me by God. That meant I didn't have to remain stuck in either society's definition of me or my own definition of me. That meant I was equipped to move beyond life's tragedies.

Because I knew the scriptures, I would rely on them to pull me through even when I was straddling the fence, struggling to love myself and to find my confidence. And pull me through they did. When I needed to develop strength about my many experiences, those I was responsible for and those I was not responsible for, I relied on Isaiah 54:17, which told me that evil would come against me, but it would not destroy me. This passage told me that I would be judged and people would talk about me, but I had the power to condemn them, and I was to condemn them. When I wanted to settle down and stop spoiling or violating my body, I relied on 1st Corinthians 6:19, which told me my body did not belong to me as is it the temple of the Holy Spirit. Talk about conviction; that behavior stopped quickly! When I felt ugly and dirty, I relied on Ephesians 1:4, which told me I was chosen before the foundation of the world that I may be "Holy and unblemished in His sight." When I questioned whether or not I was capable of completing a task or rising above my circumstances, I relied on Philippians 4:13, which reminded me that "I could do all things through Christ who strengthened me." When I battled with internal fury and turmoil I relied on Philippians 4:7 and remembered that I could tap into the peace of God because it passed all understanding and would keep my heart and mind. When I did not think abundant living was for me, I relied on John 10:10, which told me the thief cometh not, but to steal and to kill and to destroy but Christ came that I might have life, and here is what really spoke to me, not just that I might have life abundantly, but that I might have life more abundantly. When I did not feel I could go on, I relied on Isaiah 40:31, which told me that because I had trust in the Lord my strength would be renewed. I would soar on wings like eagles; I would run and not get weary and I would walk and not faint.

God's story gave me a very different perspective of who I was and how important I was. After digesting His story, I would no longer worry about the attacks and challenges, for I knew they would come, but I also knew they would not kill me. I relished the fact that I was so important to Him that, regardless of what I had done, I was unblemished in His eyes. It brought me great joy to know I was created to operate in a limitless space through Him. As a result of believing His story, I learned to treat my body as the temple it was. I also learned to release that inner turmoil and embrace that peace that surpasses all understanding. I learned to leap even when I did not think I was worthy of a thing because He came that I might live more abundantly. He had given me my purpose, and He would help me see it through. He would stand by me and help me see my goals through until the end, since He was the one who had given me these goals and desires in the first place. I learned that I was chosen and no statistic or negative belief system could define me for I had been defined by my creator before either of the two, statistics or belief systems, ever existed. I am God's story, and I am sticking to it.

Chapter 7: Forgiven

Often when we think about or hear the word forgiveness we think about forgiving others. However, forgiving ourselves is just as important as forgiving others. We usually reflect on what others have done to us before we think about what we have done to ourselves. During my growth and healing process, I found that before I could forgive anyone else, I had to forgive myself. I had gotten really good at beating myself up and putting myself down. The negative self-talk was constant. During those times when I was doing well, meeting deadlines or attaining goals, my negative self would remind me of the mistakes I had made along the way. When I was feeling low, my negative self was there to validate my feelings with comments like, "I told you so." As I reminisced on past failures, no matter how much I would do, how many wins I would have or how much I grew intellectually, I could not shake the anger I felt toward myself. I was angry with myself for staying quiet and not speaking up for all those years. I was angry because I had allowed my early experiences to dictate my decision making when it came to relationships with those of the opposite sex. I was angry because I didn't value myself enough to save myself. I was angry because I had allowed others to use me. I felt as though I should have treated myself better.

Forgiveness, according to psychologists, is defined as "a conscious, deliberate decision to release feelings of resentment or vengeance toward a person or group who has harmed you, regardless of whether they actually deserve your forgiveness." I grew up hearing the scripture, "If you forgive others when they sin against you, your heavenly father will also forgive you" (Matthew 6:14). As a child I prayed the Lord's Prayer almost daily and was quite familiar with the line that says, "Forgive us our trespasses as we forgive those who trespass against us." There was no question about whether or not I was to forgive others, but nothing I'd read or heard spoke of forgiving myself.

When my children were small I would lock myself in the bathroom when I needed or wanted to be alone. Besides a few occasional knocks on the door there would be few interruptions. One evening while having my personal pity party or mini meltdown, things came to a head. The cause of the meltdown is a blur, but my feelings of deliverance and freedom remain crystal clear. The tears streamed down my cheeks. First it was due to the negative self-talk, but then there was a different voice, one I had not heard before, "God has already forgiven you, you must now forgive yourself." I nearly stopped crying to make sure I was still alone. The words pierced my soul, for I believed I had reached a turning point. Healing was underway. The forgiveness did not happen instantly or overnight; it was a process. It was a process that required me to look at the dark places I'd visited and say to myself, "If God has already forgiven me, I can forgive me." This was not easy. There were times when I had to revisit places over and over again because I was still haunted or drinking the poison. Day after day, I would find myself saying, "If God has already forgiven me, I can forgive me."

It wasn't until after I forgave myself that I could begin the process of truly forgiving others. I knew I had to forgive others to move on. I had heard of how the lack of forgiveness affects the person who was harmed more than the person who inflicted the harm. I knew how anger and bitterness can take you out physically, mentally and emotionally to such a degree that you stop living. I did not want a root of bitterness to control my life. I did not want this bitterness to affect my relationships either. I had a responsibility and a commitment to my husband and my children.

To walk in my calling to free myself from my own enslavement, I forgave. I not only forgave but I also found compassion. I forgave my mother for the physical, emotional and verbal abuse she'd administered. I found compassion for her as she too had suffered a great deal of pain early in life and did the best she could with the information she had. I forgave my father for abandoning me and not being there to protect me from the hands of the perverted men that entered my life and touched my body. I found compassion for, like my mother, he too suffered early in life and did the best he could with the information he had. I forgave the men who molested me. I found compassion as I questioned what must have been going on inside of them, how they must have felt about themselves and how damaged they must have been to conduct themselves in such a manner. I forgave the various teachers who spoke ill words into my life. I found compassion knowing that misery loves company. I do not believe a happy, full functioning adult in his or her right mind can inflict pain on an innocent child. I forgave so many about so much. I found compassion for them all. I had reached a place of knowing that people can only give what they have. Unfortunately, that includes pain, hurt, anger and hatred. I had to forgive so that I could live.

If we are unable to forgive ourselves, we become stagnant. Since we cannot erase or undo our past actions, we become stuck in a bitter cycle of denial, shame and regret. Forgiveness towards others is a difficult path, but forgiveness towards self is often even more difficult. In order to forgive, we have to acknowledge past deeds and go face to face with the past. However, forgiveness is also one of the most beautiful journeys there is and is most worthwhile. Forgiveness creates an openness, a desire to leave the past in the past and move forward with open arms. Once our arms have been opened, they can be filled with goodness.

Haunted by Dead Demons
"I'm going to take these off. Sshhhh you have to be very quiet," he whispered after waking me in the

middle of the night. I didn't know what Uncle D was doing. I did not know he was acting inappropriately. He then prompted me to move from my bed to the floor. My tiny body lay on the floor, gown raised up over my head, panties off, being used as his pleasure doll. His adult body lay next to mine as he rubbed his penis on my private parts. He would then touch my parts with one hand while holding his with his other hand. His body would begin to shake, he would breathe heavily and then it would end. "Put your panties back on and don't tell anyone. If you do, I'm going to get in trouble. Do you want me to get into trouble?" he asked. We returned to our beds. I lay in mine in a state of bewilderment while he lay in his fast asleep. In the beginning, these activities would only take place once a week, but at some point the frequency increased. It became a part of my nightly bedtime routine. I'd put on my night clothes, brush my teeth, say my prayers, climb into bed and fall asleep. Sometime before day break I'd be awakened with a shake and the words "take your panties off." This would go on every night I was at my mother's house until we moved from 38th avenue to Paxton. Uncle D didn't move with us to the new apartment. I often wondered if someone knew what was taking place.

Uncle D was arrested soon after the police left our house. They asked questions such as when it happened and how. They wanted details about positioning and everything. I answered them to the best of my ability. I never saw Uncle D again. He was the brother of my mother's boyfriend.

Although, now knowing it was wrong for an adult man to touch my privates, cousin Ray, who was the nephew of my mother's boyfriend, wasn't quite a man yet, and, besides, his advances were not as overt as Uncle D's were. Cousin Ray liked to wrestle when the adults left us children home alone. His wrestling always led to me being pinned down with him on top of me. One day the game changed from wrestling to hide and seek. He lived in a large, three-story home in the Oakland Hills with his parents and siblings. I found him hiding on the bottom level of the home in an area that was rarely used by the adults. After finding him, the game changed, and my confusion returned. He was playful as he placed my hand on his exposed private parts. He became aggressive as I turned to run away. He grabbed my arm with a firm grip and threatened to hurt me if I told anyone. I never told.

"When you turn 12 I can put it inside of you." Of the three unfortunate events, these words still affect me in some kind of way from time to time.

These were the words of my stepfather, someone who entered our lives and home shortly after the last boyfriend. He was a really nice-looking man according to the comments the ladies made when he came to the apartment complex to visit his sister. He was brown skinned with long curly hair, 6'4" and very muscular, like many guys who are released from jail after a long period. I'm sure my mother thought she had won a prize when he chose her over the other women who were also salivating over him, but with his presence came much pain.

Initially, he was very nice and caring. I remember liking him because I knew he could protect us after I stood and watched him pummel a man outside of our front door and threaten one of the neighborhood boys who'd been picking on me. However, his heroic act required payment. Shortly after having a talk with that boy, he began asking my mother to let me stay home from church. She'd go to church and we would play house. He would have me climb on top of him and ride him until he came. Every Sunday that I wasn't with Nanny, which became less frequent at his promptings, I was home with him, clothes off, legs straddled across his large body sliding up and down on his penis. His protection is what kept me quiet. By now I knew this was wrong, but he was kind to me, and he protected me from my mother. When he was home he always found a way to stop her from yelling at me or hitting me. I was willing to stay home on Sundays if it meant the rest of my days at her house were going to be peaceful.

The thought of his behavior and plans is disturbing, even today. The thought that he planned to go further or "put it in" two years later meant he had no plans of discontinuing his actions. The fact that he was waiting for me to turn 12 makes me wonder if he thought that would be a good age to cover up his crime with the lie that I had become sexually active or if he believed my body would then be mature enough to accept his adult parts. Whatever was going on in his mind, he was devising a plan. His actions were premeditated. If he felt any guilt or remorse for his actions, he didn't show it.

Of the three incidents, the third left the darkest stain and created the most pain. This may have been because I was older and had an awareness of what was transpiring, or it may have been because those encounters taught me about sexual activities. I was more involved and instructed on how to perform. I can't say for certain why, but I struggled the most over my exchanges with my stepfather more than any other. In addition to having my thoughts and beliefs about sex shaped, my belief and ability to trust others was also shaped.

Today I am unaware of the whereabouts of uncle D or cousin Ray. My stepfather died a few years ago. In my mind they were all dead, but until recently their demons continued to haunt me. Their demons showed up in my marriage if my husband touched me a certain way. They showed up in my parenting as no one was exempt from being viewed as a predator. They showed up in platonic relationships as I questioned everyone's motive, believing if they did something nice for me surely they were looking for something in return. They showed up in my mind as I relived the events every so often. I was haunted internally when I'd judge myself for not telling as I looked in the mirror. I was haunted until I made the decision to attack their demons the only way I knew how, with God by my side. "God has not given us a spirit of fear, but of power and of love and of a sound mind" (2nd Timothy 1:7).

In a way, our demons never disappear. It's naive to pretend that we can forget what happened to us or pretend that it never happened. First and foremost, we must acknowledge the pain that we've gone through. We must validate our feelings and the fact that we were wronged. However, acknowledging our demons doesn't mean succumbing to them. The demons will continue to show up until you confront them head on, but it's important that you don't do that alone. Ask God for his aid, to walk by your side. Open up to friends, family, people you know that you can trust. Choose your weapon to attack the demons and pray for guidance to prepare an attack plan. I have found that the more you stand up to and confront the demons the smaller they become, and you slowly disempower them. Confronting your past isn't easy, but I promise you it's worth it.

Don't Drink the Poison

It is said that refusing to forgive someone is like drinking poison and expecting the other person to die. Some would argue against this statement, noting that it places blame on the victim or that the ability to forgive is emotional or comes from our emotions and that we can't control our emotions. I would have to respectfully disagree. One of my favorite sayings is, "We get to choose." We get to choose our response to everything that happens to us. When something bad is done to us or if someone wrongs us by inflicting pain, we get to choose. We can either choose to dwell on it, allowing it to eat away at us, make us bitter and live inside our internal prison, or we can face it head on, accept it as an event in life and let it go. I realize this is not the easiest or most convenient approach, but after living with and being bound by confusion, anger, lack of trust and bitterness for so many years, I have found it to be the most freeing approach.

Until I chose to forgive, I remained under the control of those events and individuals who had victimized me. While I was not physically held captive by them, I was held captive mentally and emotionally. All of my decisions were made from an unhealthy place. I overreacted to the most minute situations, blowing things up unnecessarily, living under the auspices that if one person did me wrong, I was not going to allow anyone else to do me wrong or make me wrong. I drank the poison called unforgiveness, and it was robbing me of the abundant life I was supposed to be living. Although I was awake or appeared awake on the outside, the poison was slowly killing me on the inside. If I didn't do something about it, it was going to destroy me and a lot of my relationships along with it.

This path to forgiveness has been and continues to be explored by many: the long term employee who was laid off due to a downsize or reorganization, the loyal and committed spouse or significant other whose partner was disloyal and not so committed, the parent who "trained up the child the way it should go" (Proverbs 22:6) only to later watch the child choose a different way, the person who accepted physical and or verbal abuse in the name of love, the business partner who was swindled out of his or her share, the unloved child, etc. The path is riddled with poison and overcrowded with individuals who have been betrayed in one way or another. The individuals found on this path have unknowingly allowed their hurt and sadness to turn into a hardness. Most are easily identified by the scrawl worn on their faces, their cynical attitude or their argumentative nature. They are the individuals who are defined by the story of their past and readily share it given an opportunity, welcomed or unwelcomed. They are the individuals who find themselves alone at the end of life because their venom has driven everyone away. They allow their past to define them and let their circumstances dictate who they are.

Mother Teresa said, "If we really want to love we must learn how to forgive." Martin Luther King, Jr., said, "Let no man pull you low enough to hate him." Mahatma Gandhi said, "The weak can never forgive. Forgiveness is the attribute of the strong." We know all three of these great people suffered and were publicly ostracized, but each went on to become respected by nations for their works and character. Their position on forgiveness tells of their character and level of freedom. They had a lot to be bitter about or hardened by, but instead they forgave. They moved on. Because they were able to forgive, they were able to focus on their missions. They were not bound by negative thoughts and emotions. It was their freedom and optimism that kept them moving forward, that caused them to persuade and convert people who did not believe in what they were doing and that allowed them to form a community and movement that would forever change the world.

"Forgiveness doesn't excuse the behavior. Forgiveness prevents their behavior from destroying your heart."- Unknown

The Secret Sauce

For years I prayed for peace. A few years ago, the answer to my prayer showed up in the most un-profound way. As I sat creating business cards for my coaching practice, I typed the words "choose to live an amazing life" for the tag line. A few days later I created the following quote: "In this life we get to choose, so choose to live an amazing life." I wanted people to know that no matter what happens or has happened they could choose to live amazingly. From that quote, the word "choose" became the premise for not only many of my teachings but also for my life. Something went off inside of me. No longer did I have to be controlled by circumstances. When I owned the fact that I got to choose, my thinking shifted completely, and I became a different person. I was genuinely happier and more at peace. I could not believe the answer to my prayers would be found in one word, "choose." It was so simple but so powerful. In one word I found everything I had been searching for for so many years.

I know it sounds too simple to be true or really work, but I assure you it does. With every situation I tell myself, "You get to choose." I remind myself that I get to choose my next move. I get to choose to fly off the handle in an immature, angry rage or to remain calm and handle things as an intelligent adult. It is my choice. Think about it, how much freer would you feel if you owned your actions? Take responsibility over your life. You hold the power; you hold all the tools that you need.

Upon first adopting this practice, I used the word or phrase every time I got the chance. It was embedded in my electronic signature; it was on all of my stationery. It had become a part of me so much that people would tease me, especially my staff at the time. When someone came into my office to complain about being overworked or what they did not like about the company, I would simply remind them that by complaining they were giving away their power and that they had the power to choose. They could choose to do the job they'd signed a contract for and agreed to do, or they could choose to terminate the contract and obtain employment elsewhere.

Before owning my power to choose, I carried more baggage than a departing airplane. I would get angry with my children and husband for not behaving how I thought they should behave, and I would complain about what I did not like about my job or my life. I had unfair expectations for myself and those around me. The decision to choose helped me in every area of my life. When my children did things I did not like, when my husband failed to pick up after himself, when someone cut me off while driving, I chose to remain calm. I learned that in remaining calm, I could assess things from an intellectual space rather than an emotional place. Blair Singer said, "When emotions go up, intelligence goes down." Prior to owning my power to choose, I'd often made emotional decisions. If you have not guessed it by now, the secret sauce is understanding and embracing your power to choose and understanding and believing you get to choose to live an amazing life.

After choosing to live amazingly, life still happened to me. I still had trials and tribulations such as financial setbacks when a real estate investment went bad causing us to lose $40,000. The brother of one of our tenants filed a frivolous lawsuit against us, alleging he had fallen from the porch due to a broken banister. (We later learned he broke the banister and filed the lawsuit to avoid having to pay for the damages.) Our management company stole thousands of dollars from us by way of disguised repairs. The trials and tribulations came in the form of allegations from my family who talked of how I thought I was better than them because my language and behavior was different than what they were used to. These challenges were all hard, but I chose to continue forward in what I knew was the right way to live my life. Yes, life still happened and although each experience caused some kind of emotional rise or pain, the effects of those experiences were unable to take root. Instead, I found myself analyzing each situation and searching for the lesson I was to learn. As a result, I have grown spiritually, personally and emotionally.

What does an amazing life look like for you? Is it a lower volume in your home, no chaos in your life, less worrying, decreased anxiety, reduced stress levels, improved relationships, enhanced communication, better health, more peace, more joy, more laughter? With the tools of forgiveness, friendship, determination, faith, confidence and so many others at your disposal, you can have and live that life. Don't let your past hold you back. Don't let fear hold you back. Don't let others hold you back. All you need is a willingness to do the work. You are exactly who you need to be in order to love and embrace your greatest asset and to fulfill your true purpose. Whatever an amazing life looks like for you, you can have it because in this life we get to choose, so choose to live an amazing life!

www.ingramcontent.com/pod-product-compliance
Lightning Source LLC
Chambersburg PA
CBHW072200090426
42740CB00012B/2325